Successful Teambuilding
in a week

Successful Teambuilding

in a week

GRAHAM WILLCOCKS
STEVE MORRIS

Hodder & Stoughton

A MEMBER OF THE HODDER HEADLINE GROUP

Orders: please contact Bookpoint Ltd, 39 Milton Park, Abingdon, Oxon OX14 4TD.
Telephone: (44) 01235 400414, Fax: (44) 01235 400454. Lines are open from 9.00 -
6.00, Monday to Saturday, with a 24 hour message answering service.
Email address: orders@bookpoint.co.uk

British Library Cataloguing in Publication Data
A catalogue record for this title is available from The British Library

ISBN 0 340 712074

First published 1995
Second edition 1998

Impression number	10	9	8	7	6	5	4	3	2	1
Year	2004	2003	2002	2001	2000	1999	1998			

Cover photo from Telegraph Colour Library.
Typeset by Multiplex Techniques Ltd, St Mary Cray, Kent.
Printed in Great Britain for Hodder & Stoughton Educational, a division of
Hodder Headline Plc, 338 Euston Road, London NW1 3BH by Cox & Wyman,
Reading, Berkshire.

the Institute
of Management

FOUNDATION

The Institute of Management (IM) exists to promote the development, exercise and recognition of professional management. The Institute embraces all levels of management from student to chief executive and supports its own Foundation which provides a unique portfolio of services for all managers, enabling them to develop skills and achieve management excellence.

For information on the various levels and benefits of membership, please contact:

Department HS
Institute of Management
Cottingham Road
Corby
Northants NN17 1TT
Tel: 01536 204222
Fax: 01536 201651

This series is commissioned by the Institute of Management Foundation.

■■■■C O N T E N T S■■■■

Teams obviously matter – they're an issue on every manager's agenda and in all sorts of journals and articles. They are important in all corners of the manager's world, from the everyday work that goes on no matter what, to the quality and operational initiatives that seem to appear with increasing frequency.

The trouble is that teams are one of those areas that some people assume look after themselves – put a few individuals together, call them a team and off we go. But a team is like a human being. It is born, grows up and hopefully reaches maturity. It has its own personality, its own needs and characteristics and its own pattern of development.

Presumably you wouldn't leave a young child to grow up on its own, without affection, support and leadership. If you did you could hardly blame anyone else if the person the child grew into turned out to be not exactly what you had hoped. It's the same with teams. They too need support, leadership and affection. They too need to know the answer to the question children ask most frequently – why? – and get honest answers to the other questions that arise. They too need the freedom to establish their role in life, under the guiding hand of someone more experienced.

If they develop well, everybody wins. If they don't...

Over the coming week we will explore the basic elements that make up successful teams. We will look at why they matter and why they're important – to you, themselves and the organisation. We will examine the foundations on which any effective team has to be built, and see how to build on them successfully.

Why worry?

Today is a gentle introduction to the world of teams. It is Sunday, after all, so before you launch into action tomorrow there are three questions you deserve to have answered, or confirmed, for you. The first one is simply, what are teams and what makes them different from other collections of people?

The second question is, what's in it for me? What are the benefits of teams? Why do they matter to the people in them, to me and to the organisation? Is it worth the effort?

The third is, where do I start?

Getting positive answers to these questions today will confirm your commitment to making it work.

What makes a team a team?

Every Christmas, in thousands of workplaces up and down the country, groups of people who happen to work together in the same place go off for lunch. In this group of people are some individuals who don't actually like each other very much, if at all. But they rub along throughout the year, because if they didn't the work would suffer and things could get very tense.

Then comes the season of goodwill, and the boss expects these same people to become close friends – just because they happen to have been selected for jobs that mean they have to work next to each other.

In other words, just putting six or seven people together in the same place to work does not make them a team. It makes them six or seven individuals in the same place.

You can see the same thing happening in a committee. If you have ever served on a committee you will know that, if an issue arises that leads to differences of opinion and causes two or more factions to form, a vote is taken. In mature committees the entire body of the meeting will accept this as the final corporate decision, but in most situations the group that lost the vote will try and sabotage the decision so it fails, and tell everyone outside they didn't agree in the first place.

There is certainly not one team at work here. There may be two – one for each warring faction – but this is a committee. It's not meant to be a team and there are some important differences.

Teams are special

Committees are not set up as teams. Neither are audiences, crowds or work groups. These are all just collections of people with something in common while they are together, but who aren't working to achieve a common aim. They may discuss common topics of interest, or all receive a pay packet from the same employer, but they do not have to work together.

Committees – especially those in political organisations such as central and local government – are by definition made up of opposing groups, out to defeat each other. While cynics may say that it sometimes looks as if some sports teams operate in this way – with the defence at odds with the attack – it shouldn't be like that in a team.

Changing hats

● *The management team in a medium-sized company consisted entirely of individuals who had the dual roles of management team member and head of department. Their management team meetings inevitably turned into a battle for supremacy between the different functions each manager headed – finance, marketing, operations and so on. They wanted to act more corporately, so they called in a consultant, who sat and watched.*

Her first recommendation was to scrap the management team and have head of department meetings, where it was legitimate to battle out budget, status or resource issues. Later, she said, when they recognised what teamwork really meant, they could reform the management team, and then run both types of meeting.

This example highlights precisely the difference between teams and other groups. Teams have to work together and cooperate to achieve a common aim, while other groups don't.

Horses for courses
In most organisations there is room for meetings where

- Vested interests can be put forward
- Arguments can be aired for why one department should get more money than another
- The interests of the manager's staff can be protected

and also for team meetings where

> • Those present take the wider view and work for the overall success of the organisation
> • Sectional interests are subordinate to the greater good
> • Cross-border issues are explored so departmental and functional barriers do not cloud the issues

Action point

Think critically about any teams you're involved in. Are they really teams or are they just groups? Should they be called teams or should someone rename them?

This is by no means as trivial as it might sound. People have expectations of teams and what you call something sets up expectations. If you ask individuals about teams in an organisation where the management 'team' is really a collection of departmental heads, they will tell you that the management isn't a team at all.

One tip you might find helpful is simply to call something by the name which reflects its real purpose.

Don't call it a team if it isn't, but if it should be working together for a common purpose, get the word 'team' in there somewhere. It makes a real difference to the expectations people come along with and it could make it easier for you to develop a real team approach.

In a team, everybody wins or everybody loses. In a football team you can have someone who hardly touches the ball, but they're still part of a winning team, and if the team loses, they console each other and look forward to getting a better result next time.

You can probably see in all this that there is quite a lot of unpacking to do, to get at the underlying characteristics that make this happen. There is quite a lot of work involved as well, so before you start that process off tomorrow, let's have a look at the benefits you can get from teams. After all, why should you bother unless there is something in it for you?

What's in it for me?

How would you justify the job of a manager – what's the purpose? Not, what do you do, or what are the separate skills you need, but why are there managers in the first place?

- One commonly accepted view is that management is about getting results through other people's performance. That means individuals, groups and teams.

- Imagine trying to get good results at work by dealing only with separate individuals – it just wouldn't work. It would inevitably lead to misunderstandings, different interpretations, a complete breakdown in trust and communication and very poor personal relationships. You have to work on the team as well as the individuals.

Action point

Spend a few minutes thinking of any areas where a team has the edge over an individual – where it would be more effective.

How many of the things under the following headings did you think of? What other things did you come up with?

Some things need several specialists

Unless one person has all the specialist skills and knowledge you need for a task, it pays to have a team. Of course, if any individual is able to do the whole thing it is worth considering letting them do it; teams only matter if they make a real difference and there's no point in having them just because they are in fashion.

So, if you have a task or a small project that requires some numerical skills, some practical ability and report writing talent, collect them together and build a team.

Teams reduce complexity

Imagine you want everyone to help you pack a lorry with boxes of goods. If you come to the task without having communicated as a team and worked out who does what, when and where and in what order, you are going to have to issue individual and detailed orders as the work proceeds. And, like it or not, it will almost certainly end in chaos and frayed tempers.

A team planning the process will sort out all the details with little fuss, and the operation will go smoothly.

Ideas tend to flow

Once you have more than one person thinking about a problem or an issue, ideas start to spark each other off.

Someone in the team has experienced a similar problem before, so they have particular knowledge to impart, while someone else has a fresh mind on it, so they are not limited by past experience. A creative exchange takes place, and 'brainstorming' generates unexpectedly rich input. We will return to this on Friday.

The family affair

There are emotional benefits in having teams. People start to support and encourage each other, to understand each other better and to communicate more effectively, even when they are not working together in the team. If someone has a personal problem, it can be made more manageable by talking it over with someone they trust and respect, such as a fellow team member.

People need affection and a sense of belonging, even at work. Teams can help provide this essential emotional context.

They support your training effort
Any new member joining a team should be shown the ropes and helped to make the right moves.

Imagine someone coming to your organisation from a similar job elsewhere. If your organisation is based on individuals looking after themselves, the others will stand by and watch as the newcomer fills in the wrong documents, does the wrong thing or gives a wrong answer, because that's what always happens.

In a team, though, someone will quietly come up and put them right, avoiding them and you having to sort out a potential mess.

Decisions tend to be better

No individual knows everything and – as with ideas and knowledge earlier in this list – sharing decisions can identify some ways forward you might otherwise not have thought of.

There's another benefit here as well. Most people are cooperative if they feel a sense of active participation; whereas they are likely to resist a decision taken 'on their behalf'. It doesn't matter that it's a sensible decision; what matters is that it's yours, not theirs. This does not mean you have to turn your management role into a democracy, it just means that, where appropriate and relevant, it pays to get the team's involvement in a decision.

Apart from anything else, if they have been party to the decision, their commitment rockets. Your problem may be stopping them, not getting them going. Even those who aren't entirely convinced are more willing to go along with a decision they had a hand in, and you may find them defending it to others, very unlike the committee arrangements.

What's in it for them?

So, you know what's in it for you. What about the individuals and the organisation?

As individuals
For the individuals in the team there are benefits of:

* Greater involvement and empowerment
* The chance to play a real part in decision-making and implementation
* Enhanced motivation and greater job satisfaction
* More interesting work
* The social and emotional benefits seen in the previous list

Can you see anything here that will possibly interfere with your success? Of course not, quite the opposite. Get your people experiencing these benefits and you will gain with them.

For the organisation
This probably doesn't need an answer by now. Compare two organisations, one where teams are discouraged, and one where they are encouraged.

Which one is going to be the more effective, more successful and more dynamic?

Where do I start?

Well, you don't just leap into action. The place to start is where you are now, with a clear idea of what teams really are and why they matter. Then recognise that it takes time to build and develop a team.

While you can put a group together in a few minutes, it's important to recognise that teams don't start operating at full power on Day 1. They start off as collections of individuals and they gradually form into a coherent team. Teambuilding is an evolutionary process. This is where you come in, as team leader. Your role is to help the team focus on its own development, and encourage it to grow into a mature entity, always remembering that you too are one of the team.

This is why the week is shaped as it is, with an introduction today, a look at the main issues tomorrow and a more detailed look at the key characteristics of teams daily for the rest of the week. If you can, wait until you have looked at all the topics before starting to work with the full team on any one of them. Then on Saturday you'll be invited to share your thoughts, knowledge and ideas with them, at the start of a teambuilding process.

Summary

Today, we have looked at what exactly teams are. We have examined what benefits they bring to you as a team leader and to the organisation and other team members. You are now ready to move into a more detailed exploration of what makes a successful team. We will look into those characteristics tomorrow.

How your team measures up now

Yesterday we looked at why teams are special, what sets them apart from other sorts of groups, and why teams can make all our jobs so much more successful. Today, we will check out what makes special teams special and look at how well one of your own teams is doing.

This matters for a very simple but powerful reason. If you are planning to work on improvements to the way your team operates you have to know what improvements are needed. You need to know the following three things:

1 How well *could* the team operate?
2 How is it doing *at the moment*?
3 What are the gaps between how it's doing *now* and how it *could* and *should* be doing?

Only when you know the answers to these questions can you plan the action to bridge the gaps. But you do not do this alone; it is for the whole team to work on.

The way your team could work

You know that two key issues set teams apart:

- They have a common purpose
- The members of the team have to cooperate and support each other

These apparently simple statements contain factors that highlight the difference between excellent teams and the rest. During the rest of the week, we will look at them in more detail but don't worry, you probably won't have to tackle them all.

Shortly, you will compare your team against each factor in turn. You will find that there are some where you need to put in more work than others. But first, you need to know what the factors are and what they all mean, at least in outline.

There are six factors in this list:

- Goals and objectives
- The right sort of leadership
- Complementary skills and roles in the team
- An atmosphere of honesty and openness
- Working methods that flourish in this atmosphere
- Taking stock of how well individuals and the team are doing

Goals and objectives

> An excellent team has clear and shared goals and
> objectives. Ask anyone in the team what its purpose is
> and they are able to tell you.

The question to ask is whether everyone has the same
picture of what the team is there for. It may have started out
with a clear purpose some time ago – maybe to sort out a
particular problem or complete a special project – but is that
purpose still valid? Things change over time, so have the
goals and objectives altered subtly without being clarified?

If you want people in a team to work together and cooperate for success, they have to know what they are cooperating for. Never assume that everyone else shares your picture of things. Think about your own experience as a member of a team and you will almost certainly recall times when you were unsure what you were there to do. Either you never knew because the issue wasn't addressed or the team's goals changed over time.

Whichever it was, the chances are you then invented your own version and operated on guesswork and assumption. You may even have guessed right, but guesswork can never be justified as a sound basis for making plans about an important management activity!

In an excellent team everyone knows because everyone talks about it. Telepathy is not a talent that most of us have, so it is vital that the team's goals and objectives are clear and understood by everyone involved.

The right sort of leadership

> The effective team leader is part of the team and not someone who stands outside, laying down rules or acting as an autocrat.

The leader sets the tone. There are teams everywhere in the world of sport and each team has a captain. The captain doesn't just stand about shouting at the other players, he or she plays a full part in what the team does and shares equally in success or failure. He or she listens properly to other team members and gives them support and feedback.

The captain is not the only one to congratulate, castigate or commiserate with other players and the differences between the leader and the rest just aren't always that obvious to the outsider.

So it is with teams at work. The same sort of issues exist and the way the leader behaves has just as much impact here as it does on a sports field.

Complementary skills and roles

An excellent team has all the skills it needs to achieve its purpose and this means having people with different styles, different approaches and different strengths.

If you think about what a team does, you can see there are two sides to it.

One side is 'what it does': the activities individuals carry out to get to the objectives. These often include specific skills like planning, selling or making things, and team members carry on doing these when the team is no longer in the same place at the same time. So, the team needs a mix of specific skills.

The other side is 'how it does it': the process the team uses to function properly. The team needs someone to look after its meetings and make sure they are chaired effectively, someone else to sort out details, yet another person to have a broad vision and some bright new ideas. The trouble is that no one person is going to have all these qualities.

An atmosphere of honesty and openness

> A key hallmark of an excellent team is its members'
> ability to say what they think or feel, without putting
> other people down or being put down themselves.

This one is hard. It cuts across a lot of the normal tendencies
people have when they work in organisations. The ideal
organisation has a culture with no barriers between
departments or sections, and is a place where everyone sees
themselves as part of the overall team. The flow of
information is multiple, going in all directions between
members and across the team as a whole. People serve each
other as internal customers and give and receive honest
feedback about successes and problems. But too often it
really isn't like that.

If you have ever heard people say

- Sorry, that's not my problem
- Oh, that's the engineer's job... nothing to do with me
- It's the **!@%! accounts department again!
- Don't worry about that... it's only for the sales lot

then you'll recognise what this means in reality.

The result of a culture like this is that individuals are almost encouraged to try and score points off others. This leads to a reluctance to say what they really think and an inability to listen without prejudice. It's a 'cover your back' situation, one where saying nothing means you keep your powder dry for the fight that might develop.

You probably don't need any further explanation for now; just imagine how a team would operate if each of the members carried this sort of emotional luggage into the team with them. No trust, no support and a climate of dishonesty and beating the opposition.

Working methods that flourish

An excellent team uses approaches, techniques and procedures that fit with the right sort of leadership, the climate of honesty and trust and the acceptance of a range of complementary skills and roles.

It would be a completely pointless exercise to work hard at developing a climate of openness and trust and then for you, the team leader, to storm in and tell the others what they had to do, and how.

All the other factors in the list look towards a horizon where:

- Each team member matters
- The 'boss' isn't the boss but a fellow team member
- There is mutual trust and support across the team

This means that the way the team operates – its procedures and conventions – have to reflect this. They have to be in tune rather than discordant. The deeds have to match the words.

The procedures include the way meetings are run, the way decisions are reached and the approach to handling problems. Any real difference between people's experience of the way the team actually operates on the ground and all the utterances and publicity about what a wonderfully open team it is will shine through. Reality will always override slogans.

So, the bottom line is that the procedures have to fit with the culture and values of the team.

Taking stock

> Excellent teams only stay excellent if they monitor and review what they have done and are doing as a means of aiming at continuous improvement.

It's a simple question to ask – 'how are we doing?' – but it doesn't get asked enough. You might think it's obvious, but the things under our noses are often the ones we miss. We look out beyond them and forget the basics. Staying effective in a changing world means it's a question to ask regularly and often.

The answers to the question will generally be about the team as an entity. However, they can also be about individuals who might come up with their own development needs that they want met, in order to play a more effective part in the team.

The only way to do better is to start with how we're doing now. We all learn from experience, as long as we stand still and recognise what the experience means. Someone once said that insanity is doing a second time, with increasing determination, something you have proved doesn't work.
But everyone is in danger of making assumptions and jumping into action, when the pressure is on and things get really busy.

The alternative takes a little time but it pays dividends.
Here are the steps to achieve continuous improvement:

- Reflect on what happened
- Identify why it happened
- Plan to repeat the things that worked
- Plan to avoid repeating the things that didn't
- Try out the new approach and start the process
  again from the top

How is your team at present?

Now you have confirmed what makes up an excellent team,
you can check out your own. If you do this on your own you
can get a pretty clear picture of the state of play, as long as
you:

1 Are completely honest
2 Make absolutely no assumptions; if you don't know
  for sure, don't guess
3 Are confident that everyone else sees things exactly
  as you do

You're not sure? Well, for now it's best to stick with your
own views. Over the rest of the week you will be looking at
each factor in more detail, so you could be jumping the gun
by starting a wider debate now. Just be aware of the three
points in the list above as you run through the check-list.

Action point

Pick one team that you work with. Ideally, pick one you lead but if you are still getting ready to build your first team focus on one you are a member of.

Rate the team by selecting the point on the scale where you feel it sits for each of the factors. 1 is very low indeed, or never, and 10 is perfection, or always.

Mark on a scale of 1–10

- Everyone knows exactly what the team's purpose and objectives are
- The leadership style and approach is participatory, not autocratic
- The team members between them have all the skills and attributes the team needs

- The climate is one where people are always open and honest and don't hold back
- The team meetings and discussions help us operate as a real team
- We regularly ask the question, 'how are we doing as a team?'

The next steps

Interpreting the check-list results and identifying a priority order for your team gives you a starting point for action. If you only have two or three issues in need of urgent attention, don't ignore the rest, they still matter and can always be improved, even a little.

My priorities are:
1
2
3
4
5
6

If you are already leading a team and want to make it even better, then your priority list tells you what you probably suspected, but may not have been able to quantify. The chances are that not everything is a priority. For instance, you may have clear objectives, but a climate where honesty and openness get stifled.

If you intend to build a team you now have some idea of the main areas to watch out for. In this situation you will have to pay attention to each of the factors as we go through them over the rest of the week. However, you will have started to sort out for yourself your own strengths and weaknesses with regard to leading a team. This insight will help you put your efforts in the right place.

Summary

Today, we have looked at how well your team operates *now* and how well it *could* operate. We assessed your team on the basis of its rating on six very important factors, and then prioritised the factors in which your team is weak.

Tomorrow we'll start looking in detail at what action you can take to work on your priorities.

Follow my leader

Today you are looking at two of the key characteristics of teams: leadership and purpose. Any successful team needs a leader with the skills to hold things together and a clear sense of purpose and direction.

The team leader

The first question to ask is, what makes an effective team leader? The best way of approaching this is to look at what matters to you when you are on the other side of the fence. What you value will almost certainly match what others value too, because human beings are remarkably consistent in this area.

If you think about a team where you were a member and not the leader, it might help you focus on what you valued in the characteristics and skills of the leader. Remember, this is a team, not any other group.

Which of the following do you think makes a more effective leader of a team you're in?

a Someone who is totally in control and who:
- Releases just enough information to get things done
- Keeps back quite a lot of information and data so they can take the important decisions themselves
- Tells everyone exactly what they need to do and how to do it

b Someone working in the team as a partner who:
- Shares all available information
- Encourages participation and team decision-making
- Allows people to work out the details between themselves
- Avoids trying to control everything

If you look back to what you saw yesterday, it is fairly obvious that the second set of characteristics is the right set. The first does not fit at all with a team spirit, although it might fit with groups that are not teams.

Action point

Have a look at the following ten statements and rate yourself as honestly as you can on each one. Give yourself a rating out of 50 for each one and, if possible, check out your own opinion with a friend or colleague who will give you honest feedback on how right they think you are.

- I know exactly what I want to achieve ☐
- I share my aims and objectives with the rest of the team ☐
- I am loyal to my team and its individual members and I'll defend them if someone outside has a go ☐
- I trust the team and its individual members ☐
- I like to delegate in order to help people learn and develop ☐
- I don't duck issues – I face the facts ☐
- I give credit and praise when the team does well, and honest and open feedback with respect when they don't ☐
- I get pleasure and pride from seeing the team and its members do well ☐
- I like to make sure the team has some clear guidelines to work to ☐
- I think work should be enjoyable wherever possible and that job satisfaction is important for everyone ☐

For most people these are the sorts of characteristics that make up a team leader they really respect and value. In turn, this means that the team members will work their socks off for someone like this, someone they want to do well for out of respect, rather than fear or coercion.

Fifty for each one would be nice, but unrealistic. You will have some strengths and some weaknesses so if you allow about 30 out of 50 as an acceptable level you can start to see where you might need to look at your leadership style in the team. However, even if you scored more than 30 it doesn't mean you are perfect, so avoid complacency. Just work on the biggest needs first.

Start to put together some ideas for a strategy to develop in the areas where you have most room for improvement, and consider sharing the whole issue of your leadership style with the rest of the team, maybe on Saturday. After all, they are the ones who will be most affected by the way you operate, so their views can give you valuable information.

Manager or leader?
This is an important issue to face. Management can tend to imply control, supervision and authority. Leadership on the other hand is about warmth, honesty, and developing a sense of working together.

There has been a lot of research into the differences between leadership and management and so far no one has clearly cracked the problem. But one way of looking at it is to say that you manage from above, but you can lead from the middle. Management is something that comes in the job description. Leadership is something that other people bestow on you.

If you look around your organisation and spot the leaders, you will inevitably find that they are not all the people in control at the top. It can be someone on the front line who seems somehow able to get people to work with them. It could be the person they elected as union representative, because they trust and respect them.

So leaders don't have to be managers, and they often aren't. But managers need to be leaders, if for no other reason than that they have teams to lead rather than manage. Releasing the potential of the other team members is at the heart of any effective team leader's role and this depends on trust, honesty, openness and respect, in both directions.

It may be the case that there are some natural-born leaders, who just seem able to get people to follow their lead, apparently without effort. However, most of them have worked at it as well. To become the sort of leader who can get the best from a team means work on your own style and your own approach. It means letting go of control and sharing authority, and sharing success and failure too. It isn't easy but once it starts to take off you will be so delighted by the results that it gets easier.

In the list where you looked at the 10 characteristics of a leader, a couple were about knowing what you want to achieve, and sharing that awareness with the rest of the team. Now you've started to work on your own role, this issue of aims and objectives is the first step in developing the strength of the team.

A sense of direction

The basic definition of a team we're working to is individuals working together for a common purpose, so team aims and some clear objectives are important because:

- Unless you know where you are going you can't plan and complete the journey
- Without aims and objectives, people will go off in their own direction and the team will split apart as confusion, misunderstanding and even rivalry grow
- Teams exist even when the team members aren't together. This is what is meant by the intangible 'esprit de corps'. The team does not fade away when a meeting ends; individuals carry on working for the team's aims on their own, so everyone needs to know what their role is and what their tasks are

The writing team

A word on the topic of team members working alone at times. The team that produced this book is spread all over the UK – one in Wales, another in London, the publisher in another part of London and so on.

Naturally, there were meetings to work out who did what, by when, and how team members would support and help each other. So while, for most of the time the people were not physically close, they did communicate and they were working to a common aim and some clearly understood objectives.

Having no aims or objectives would be like asking a football team to score a goal when there weren't any goal posts and the number of goals that were needed was a secret.

Knowing where you're going
Most of us have been in a team where we weren't completely sure of what the team was there for or why it was there. Like people, teams aren't immortal, and this vague directionless feeling usually occurs when a team has outlived its founding purpose.

One simple way of looking at this issue is to think about meetings you go to, where you are a member of a team rather than its leader.

Action point

Think about a team you have worked in where there wasn't a clear purpose and consider how it made you feel and how effective it was at getting results.

You probably remember how often you and the other team members groaned about even having to go to meetings because they seemed to have no purpose and certainly achieved nothing. As you shuffled in to meet the rest of the team, you and they probably muttered, 'I don't see the point', or 'Why are we doing this?' As soon as you get to this level of non-excitement, the team is either dead or in need of resuscitation; it's pointless letting it struggle on in the dark with no commitment.

Now put yourself in the shoes of a team you lead and reflect on how clearly they know what is expected of them. Do not assume they must know just because you do!

If there aren't clear aims for a team to work to there are two probable reasons:

- There simply aren't any. Either there never were or there may have been some once, but they have been lost in the mists of time as some of the objectives have been achieved
- Assumptions are being made about what everybody understands

Before the start of your next team meeting write down on a piece of paper what you see as the purpose of the team – what is it there to achieve. Then at the start of the meeting get the other team members to write down their versions, on their own, and afterwards compare the results. The similarity or difference will give you something very valuable to discuss on Saturday, when you open up the debate with the rest of the team.

If there is any doubt or confusion, the responsibility for clarifying the aims rests with you. It is the team leader's job to make sure that everyone is explicitly and consciously working for the same broad aims. However, don't invent aims for the sake of it. If the team was set up to do something it has completed, wrap it up with a celebration and concentrate on teams with something important left to do.

Aims and objectives

While you know it is important to let the team make decisions and to plan its own operations as far as possible, it is you who decides to set up a team in the first place because there is something you think it can do. Here is that crucial leadership function we have already considered. At the very start you know what the team's aims are and they don't.

Action point

Think of a team you set up fairly recently. What was the aim? What did you want it to achieve?

This aim is the broad target you set, probably even before you picked the people you thought would make the right team. So the first issue to sort out when you have everyone in the same room – assuming they know each other and don't need much introduction – is why they are there.

The reason we are working as a team is that we need to...

Stop there. Let it sink in with the team.

Then start to turn it over to them. Ask a question and sit back.

How do you think we could go about this?

Once the discussion gets going, some steps on the way to success will start to come out.

Well, we need to get the paperwork organised.

Yes, and the accounts department needs to know what we're up to, because it affects them.

Perhaps the main thing is to get the locations for the machines sorted out and arrange the power supply.

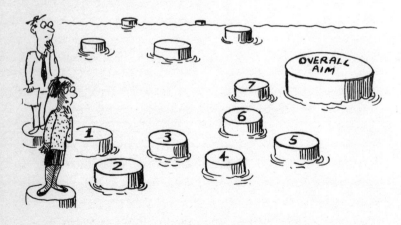

Whatever emerges can be turned into objectives – more detailed steps along the way to the overall aim. Objectives are an essential starting point, often written so they say:

The objective is to ...(specify exactly what is to be done) ... by ... (whenever it is needed).

However, you may need a bit more than the bare objective. Have you ever been to a meeting where an argument started when you asked Bill how something was going – in the belief Bill was handling it – and Bill says it had been a job that Jim had said he'd handle? Jim recalls quite distinctly that it had been given to Joyce... who claims to know nothing about it. If you have, you will know that it is a time-consuming waste of energy.

Whether individuals or small teams from the big team are going to tackle certain steps, there has to be some way of ensuring everyone knows what they and their counterparts are doing, and what the constraints – deadlines, resource limits and so on – are. There are some simple words that can help here:

- What?
- Why?
- Who?
- How?
- Where?
- When?

Consider constructing a simple form with these words on it, so that for each of the steps along the way, for each objective, you can specify as a team exactly what is to be achieved and by when. Not only does it avoid confusion at the start, it also gives you something to use as a measure as progress unfolds. If one key objective is slipping you can focus on it when you review progress and take corrective action.

Summary

As you come to the end of Tuesday you have made a start on two of the key issues in teams: your leadership, and the direction the team is heading in. You won't have sorted everything out yet, but remember that Saturday is reserved for putting all the issues together and reviewing where you stand.

Tomorrow, you will look at another of the key issues: what role you want other people to play in the team, so they carry their share of the weight and support you in your job of leading.

The sum of the parts...

Today, you are looking at the roles individuals play in the team, not only their specialist roles but their roles as team players as well. A team is not just a number of individuals. It's a machine operating as a complete entity, using a range of components and parts. In the team, these components are people.

Think about a bicycle and you can see that it works because there is a whole range of different components: wheels, pedals, a frame, handlebars and so on. Some components look shiny and some, like the saddle, should make you feel comfortable. The chain on the other hand is probably greasy, and you don't really like getting your hands on it. But you can't operate effectively without a chain.

Team composition is the same. There will be some people who play a part you are very comfortable with, and others you find difficult to handle, who make you feel uncomfortable. There are two sides to this in teams:

- The right technical mix of skills, **what** the people do as specialists
- The right mix of team skills, **how** they operate to add value to the process of being a team

The right technical mix

This is a relatively straightforward issue. It comes down to having specialist skills in place to cover the technical tasks that have to be completed en route to achieving the aim.

Action point

If you were setting up a team to turn the waste plot at the front of the main office into a feature garden, what sort of technical skills would you want people to bring to the team?

You would probably want to include individuals who knew about:

- Horticulture, so you could use their expertise on what to plant where, and to ensure the right soil conditions

- Plant and machinery, so that any excavation could be handled by someone who knew which machines to use and how to operate them
- Electricity and wiring, to handle the power supply to the lights and the fountain
- Plumbing, to sort out the water supply
- Finance, to help keep an eye on the costs against the budget

All these people may not be available though, so you would have to compromise and find the best mix of skills you could. That's life; nobody promised it would all be perfect. Maybe you don't have access to specialist trades like machinery, electrical contracting and plumbing, in which case you may plump for someone with experience of selecting and managing outside contractors. Whatever you end up with, the mix will be as appropriate as you can get it – it's common sense.

It doesn't stop there

So, you have six or seven people with specialist skills in the same place at the same time. Are they a team? Not yet. This is where you started, on Sunday.

What makes them a team? Working together for a common aim – the basic definition again. You need the individuals you selected to take a wider view of the whole project and

share ownership of the overall aim. Each one is not there
just because they can drive a digger, make a watertight joint
or add up figures. Ultimately each individual is there to
contribute something less tangible – the magic that turns the
group into a team.

Milchester Rovers 1   England 0

*Bobby Robson, the ex-England football manager was asked on TV
what the main differences were between managing a club side and
managing the national team.*

*His main point was that at club level the individual players were
not necessarily the best specialist goalkeeper, strikers and
defenders in the world. But they knew each other, worked on
strategies together and understood almost instinctively what*

*someone would do in a certain situation. This team dimension
added to the skills they already had. There was no room for a 'star'* N.B.
who didn't fit in with the team.

*At national level, although he had the best players in the country,
they had only a few days together and it was infinitely harder to
get that extra magic that meant they worked as a real team.*

So, back to the garden team. If you tell them the aim – to get
a feature garden built within six months inside a budget of
£XX – and then turn them loose to sort out the objectives, the
chances are they will all pick up their natural technical roles
automatically. The finance person won't ask someone else to
handle the figures while they drive the digger and the
horticulturist won't suggest someone else looks after the
planting because they want to do the wiring. They know
what to do.

So the 'what' of the team roles looks after itself, if you chose
the people correctly. The 'how' needs a little bit more
attention.

Complements, not clones
The issue here is what individual team members do to help
the team achieve success. What difference does their
behaviour and their approach make to the way the team
operates?

Action point

If you had the chance to appoint someone as your assistant, would you choose someone exactly like you or someone different? Why?

This is a subtle feature of team relationships. Many people choose people who are like them to work with, cloning themselves. It makes life comfortable. But it isn't the best approach. You end up with two people doing the same things and nobody filling in the gaps.

On the other hand, if you chose someone different you could select someone who would:

- Do the things you didn't like
- Fill in the gaps where you were not entirely competent and confident
- Complement you in the things you were good at
- Have their own role rather than duplicate yours
- Bring another perspective to ideas and decisions

Nobody can be good at absolutely everything. You don't see sports teams where the players are interchangeable, equally skilled at defending and attacking.

An effective team is made up of individuals with their own strengths and weaknesses and the secret is to put together a team that has all the potential weaknesses covered somewhere, so you have a full range of strengths. By definition this means avoiding cloning, making sure that there are some very different characters in the team who may not feel comfortable with each other at first.

As leader, it is important you pick people – or develop the roles of those already in the team – who match up with some classic characteristics that make for an effective and rounded team. There is a cast of characters who together make up a well-rounded team.

The creative thinker
This individual comes up with some weird and wonderful ideas, sometimes when you're in the middle of something else! Their brain always seems to be on the lookout for other ways of doing things. They aren't always very good at making their ideas work and looking after the detail, but where would the team be without ideas and sharp flashes of insight?

The action person

Here is someone who never comes up with a new idea but takes someone else's idea and turns it into reality. They quietly work away at the detail and make sure it gets done. Their character means they need to know what the outcome might look like before they start work, but once they're off they will do a great deal of the work, or make sure it gets done. Clearly, this individual is very different from the creative thinker, but they work very well together as long as they both are on the same team and working to the same ends.

The pusher

This is the person who looks at their watch and reminds you there's only half an hour left and still a lot to do. They push for action and don't really like all that thinking and planning. This is helpful because it can keep the momentum going, but it can be annoying to the other team members who relish the detail and the creative process for its own sake.

The scrutineer

In the middle of an exciting discussion about how an objective can be achieved, the scrutineer looks up from the data and says you can't afford it, or it would mean more work elsewhere because of the knock-on effect. They bring you down to earth with a bump by always having their feet very firmly on the ground and coming up with the practicalities, problems and difficulties. This can be extremely difficult if you are a creative thinker, but it does stop the team going down paths of fantasy.

The smoother

This is generally someone who hates conflict and argument, so they try and mediate between opposing factions and find some common ground. They really care about the people in the team and work hard to make sure everyone feels all right, even when it is a little unrealistic. However, they act as a sort of mirror that reminds everyone to stay civilised and humane, and in doing so, perform a very valuable function for the team as a whole.

The stinger

This is someone everybody thinks at times is rude, abrasive and awkward. They confront other people directly and come up with all sorts of moral and practical arguments to explain why they wouldn't even start from here! They certainly liven up team meetings and get the adrenaline flowing, which in itself is a valuable alternative to just drifting along with the tide of opinion. But in doing so, they can offend, irritate and intimidate their colleagues, but their contribution is often extremely sensible. However, it can get ignored because the other people don't listen to what is being said, they're too busy getting angry with the stinger.

The conductor

Here is the person who keeps time and ensures everyone is in tune, managing the process of team meetings and making sure people have the chance to speak and be heard. He or she watches the way things are going and reflects back what has been said. They summarise from time to time and act like an effective chairperson in a meeting. Without this, individual meetings may never achieve their purpose and the quieter individuals such as the scrutineer, may never get a word in edgeways and give up trying.

Action point

Write down the names of the people in a team you lead. In your mind, picture them and the way they behave and decide which character(s) they are in the list above.

Hopefully you have a fair spread. You need neither too many of one type or none of another, because if you have the wrong mix there will be some weaknesses left uncovered and too much strength in other areas. The team just won't balance.

The problem is that you may not have had the chance to pick the team. This means that you may need to discuss team roles with the individuals concerned and find out whether there are hidden talents you can draw on. Always remember that the team will be built of different but, hopefully, complementary parts, and it's the *overall dynamic* that will determine its success, or otherwise.

This is especially crucial with some of the characters. For example, getting everyone to see that the stinger is not just a sheer bloody nuisance but someone who benefits the team isn't always easy, but it does repay the effort. You could give them the descriptions of the cast of characters and get them to say how they see their team. It starts them talking about the issues and helps weld the team together.

And, if someone else turns out to be a better conductor than you are, how about letting them chair some meetings? This is perhaps too radical a suggestion for many people, because the chair is traditionally associated with the person with the greatest authority. But if your own natural approach is to be a creative thinker or a pusher then the chances are you and the team will lose out in two ways:

1 It's harder to manage the process effectively and you won't get the best from the rest of the team; the results the conductor should get, just won't appear

2 The natural talents you do have will be lost or diluted as you try and adopt a role that you don't like, while someone who is a natural is sitting there trying to do a different job or just opting out.

Summary

There is a lot to today's topic. We have seen that the make-up of the team is not just a simple matter of gathering the right number of people together. Rather, it depends on the right mix of skills, behaviour and approach, and an awareness of the importance of the other people's roles across the whole team. Behind it all is your leadership role, encouraging this whole area of differences to be seen as a positive benefit and not a blockage to progress.

To be honest...

Remember what you read on Monday?

> *A key hallmark of an excellent team is its members' ability to say what they think or feel, without putting other people down or being put down themselves.*

Teams are people, and people are emotional

When teams are working at peak performance they are emotional entities. They need to operate in a climate of mutual support and trust so that, even if two team members hold entirely opposing views, they never reach the point where the disagreement gets personal. In the same way, if one member feels upset or disappointed at something a colleague has done, they need to be able to say what they think or feel, and expect to be heard. It doesn't follow that anyone else will agree with them, but the open exchange of views, opinions, values and ideas is healthy and constructive.

For individuals to make a worthwhile contribution they have to feel valued and listened to, even if they don't always get their own way. They have to feel other people want to hear from them.

Action point

Think about a meeting you have been at, where someone either sneered at an idea you put forward or simply ignored you. Maybe you tried to put your point across and someone else just talked across you. How did that make you feel about yourself, the rest of the team, and your future role?

The chances are you felt some extreme emotions: anger, resentment, frustration, and a desire to get your own back. Or else you sighed sadly and gave up. Neither of these is at all helpful when it comes to a successful team, because the next natural reaction is to come away and promise yourself you'll keep quiet next time, or you'll get your own back. But you're not alone in feeling like this. Everyone else does as well, especially characters like the smoother, the action person and the scrutineer.

The communication trap

Without a climate of trust and respect, individuals can fall into the communication trap and stop communicating effectively as instead they:

- Hold back from making contributions – so they feel frustrated and left out, and the whole team misses out on their ideas and views

- Sit on emotions that eat away at them afterwards, leading to mutual dislike and mistrust that shows up in deliberate actions and negative body language
- Go their own way and plan secret approaches at odds with what the rest of the team is aiming for

The bottom line is that if this happens, dissatisfaction starts to spread and real issues get buried. Clearly, this undermines team effectiveness. Helping them avoid the communication trap certainly makes people feel warm and comfortable, and only if they do feel good about themselves and the contribution they make, will they act as a team, not a group.

Here's an important tip: always try – like the manager in the next example – to work on teambuilding at the start of the team's life. It allows you to encourage good habits, instead of having to undo existing bad ones, that are often hard to shift and quite deep-rooted.

Shipwrecked!

The marketing manager in a small packaging firm was setting up a small project team. They all knew each other from a previous project, which hadn't gone very smoothly. The marketing manager asked the head of personnel and training to sit in on the first meeting and give them some tips to help develop the team approach.

The head of personnel used the first hour of their meeting for an exercise – a scenario where the team was supposed to have been shipwrecked, and had to work together on an escape strategy – you may know the sort of thing. When he gave his feedback on what had happened, and why they had come up with a strategy that meant they were all dead, he made the following observations.

First, he said, the team balance was way off: three pushers, one smoother, a creative thinker – who happened to be the marketing manager – and a stinger. No one acted as conductor and managed the process.

The 'pushers' had tried to take control and had jostled for supremacy, hogging the discussion and blocking anyone else, especially the quieter types, from making their points. The stinger hadn't joined in at all.

The pushers said if the others wanted to say anything they should have, which angered the quieter ones. They said they had tried to make a contribution but were always ignored, told to hang on a minute, or were told they were wrong, so they gave up, leant back in their chairs and opted out. The stinger just said it was a shambles and he wanted nothing to do with it. Some increasingly personal and hurtful comments were thrown around: 'you never bloody listen anyway – you're just a bully', and 'people like you have to be led by someone strong like me, or you'd never get it sorted'.

Now, the important issue in this example is not whether the team concerned got the right answer. As it happens they didn't, which does tell you something about the way they operated. They could always have come up with the right answer by mistake, but that's no way to run an effective team. What really matters is the way they behaved to each other. They were meant to be on the same side, working together to save themselves and their colleagues from a watery grave.

Instead, they fell straight into the communication trap.

Action point

Ask yourself, does this example ring any bells with you, from your own experience? The chances are that it does, so think about how people's behaviour needs to change, if they are to operate properly as a team.

The answer is simple: they need to avoid doing all the things that lead to the communication trap. This means they have to stick to the points in the checklist below.

Avoiding the communication trap checklist

- Listen to other people's contributions and remember – listening is an active process, it isn't the same as waiting for your turn to speak
- Accept that you aren't the only one with feelings, who gets hurt – everyone does, so put yourself in their shoes and don't take it personally or make it personal

- Recognise the importance of all the other team members and the roles they play – accept that a stinger is making a positive contribution and accept that a quiet individual may need encouragement to speak their mind
- Deal with the facts, not the individual – if you disagree with a point of view say 'I disagree with the point of view', not 'That's stupid'
- Respond, don't react – think for a couple of seconds before you launch in with a personal counter-attack, especially when it is someone whose team role is very different from yours

However, making this happen isn't so simple. There are some key steps that the team needs to go through if every member is going to communicate effectively and avoid the communication trap.

A four step approach to making it happen

The steps needed to make it happen are these:

1 Gain acceptance from everyone that there are potential dangers, or room for improvement
2 Make everyone responsible for their own actions in solving the problem or stopping one developing
3 Identify and agree some ground rules for fair play
4 Make sure everyone sticks to them, and remind them if they slip.

Using all four steps
You have to cover all four points. It is vital that everyone understands exactly what the dangers are and shares ownership of the issue. Then, when they work out ways of preventing problems arising, it is *their* solution to *their* problem in *their* team and they will all have a stake in making it work. Try and impose *your* solution and it won't stick. This is the issue of 'active participation' that we first discussed on Sunday. It's simple psychology, but it is important.

Steps 1 and 2
To cover steps 1 and 2 you could, either on your own or with the support of the people who manage your training:

• Explain the issue of openness, honesty and trust in teams, as it is set out in this book, to set the scene
• Give the team a simulated task to do – there are lots of them available commercially or you could devise your own, such as redesign the car parking or plan a new form or a new system

- Ideally, video the exercise, or get one of the team members to sit outside the team and watch what happens, using the check-list to assess how things go
- Make key notes on a board as you ask people at the end individually:
  - what happened
  - how they feel and felt, emotionally, and why
  - what they think went well
  - what they think went badly
- Either play the video or get feedback from the observer and confirm the points everyone feels could be improved

It is guaranteed that there will be several things that do go well, and these are important. If you start feedback by saying what went well, people are far more ready to hear about what didn't.

It's even more guaranteed that there will be things that go wrong – examples of the communication trap. By identifying these themselves the team – including you – will draw up their own agenda of things to be tackled.

Step 3
Remember the tip about getting teambuilding going at the start of the team's life? Well, here it is important because it lets the team sort out and clarify some ground rules before they get into detailed and possibly heated discussion on real and important tasks.

You need to let the team draw up its own ground rules, but you could start by giving them something to play around with. The following is one set of rights and responsibilities that you could use to get the ball rolling:

Everyone in this team has the right to:
- Express views and opinions, however unpopular
- Be listened to without interruption and with respect
- Say no or yes without feeling guilty
- Change their mind
- Say they don't know or they don't understand

Everyone in this team has a responsibility to:
- Accept that other people are different but equal
- Behave appropriately
- Look for strengths, not weakness in other people
- Listen to others' opinions with an open mind
- Avoid causing emotional injury or hurt

Ending up with a similar set of rights and responsibilities is one way of clarifying the ground rules.

Another approach is to describe what is required behaviour, so the list could be on the lines of:

- When one person is talking, all others must listen until they have finished
- Someone wanting to make a contribution must be allowed to do so, without someone else jumping in
- When speaking, always own your comments, and use 'I feel' or 'I think' rather than 'We feel' or 'That is', because it focuses the speaker and helps them make sure they say what they really mean

Once the ground rules have been established and agreed by everybody, you have a set of working guidelines that can be applied, monitored and policed.

Step 4
This operates at two levels: the immediate and the reflective. The immediate level may be in a team meeting where the conductor – you or whoever it is – has to watch the process and stop someone breaking the rules. In meetings it can be a simple matter of saying something like:

Pat, hang on a minute, Lyn hasn't finished.

Pat, hang on a minute. Lyn, you looked like you were going to say something?

Because you are enforcing everybody's rules, there will be no animosity and very little argument.

The reflective level is where you use some of the techniques from Steps 1 and 2, reviewing what happened and continuing to learn and improve the way things are done. This is the whole point of Saturday's look at reviewing.

The cultural pull

What if you are trying to set up an open, honest and trusting team, in an organisation where this is just not the way it works? What if the organisation has huge departmental barriers and there is a culture of blame and unhealthy competition, the sort of culture where the 'management team' is really a battleground for heads of department?

Don't tell them the whole story or they'll know as much as we do.

We stuffed the others in that meeting – I got their budget reduced and ours increased.

Send a memo – just to cover your back!

> ### Action point
>
> If your work environment feels anything like one where you might hear quotes like these, think about what difference it makes to your own team, especially if the team is made up of individuals from different parts of the organisation.

Perhaps the key thing is that the people in the team will naturally be more suspicious of an open and honest approach, if they are not used to this sort of culture. It might take a little more time to get everybody trusting everybody else. The bottom line though, is that you should only bother to try and change things you have any chance of changing, and you alone will not change the organisation's culture.

However, you can change the behaviour of your team members, so, once you start making progress, forget the culture. Somewhere, at some time, what you achieve in your team will be held up as a model of what can be done with the right approach, and then you will have done your bit to change the rest of the world.

Summary

Today, we have considered the people in the team. There are many potential pitfalls when different personalities are put together, but with careful preparation these can be avoided and personality clashes avoided. To do this we set out a four stage process which will help avoid the communication trap.

Not only do individual personalities create difficulties but the personality of the organisation might be a problem too. Remember, you might not be able to change the organisation's culture overnight, but developing your team culture could be the first step along the way.

This issue of openness, honesty, trust and respect is perhaps the hardest of all to crack, simply because it is about personal communication and everyone thinks they communicate pretty well. This is often reinforced in the way procedures are set up, the topic for tomorrow.

It's not what you do...

So far during the week you have established that teams are special and that they:

- Depend on effective leadership and clear aims
- Bring together a blend of some very different skills
- Need people to communicate openly and honestly

Today, we will focus on an issue that builds on all these things – the way the team works to achieve its aims and objectives through procedures for discussion and decision-making. It's a practical day, full of ideas and activities you can use to develop procedures that work best in your team.

It is important to establish ways of operating that fit the team and make use of all the work you have done so far, using their joint potential and enhancing the way each member is going to be involved and play a full part. It's also important to make sure they don't all look to you as their team leader every time there is a decision to be made, or when the team needs to plan its next steps. Bear in mind that biting your tongue can at times be the most valuable contribution you make. Appropriate procedures involve everyone in ideas, information and decisions. The three techniques we look at today can help start that process off.

People work best when they are feeling enthusiastic about the process. Any procedure in a team should not only be worthwhile, it should be satisfying, even fun, and you can prove this if you try out the following team techniques as 'party games'. They work just as well.

Two or more heads are better than one

One of the benefits of teams is that ideas tend to flow. Having put together a team:

- With the right mix of skills
- That knows what its job is
- Where you provide effective leadership, from the middle of the team rather than as a 'boss'
- With people communicating openly and honestly

you have all the components for a technique called 'brainstorming' which can give you an excellent range of ideas. It also works when you are trying to find all the possible causes of a difficulty, or are looking for solutions to problems.

Brainstorming

Brainstorming is a technique which you may have heard about. It helps break down the restrictive approach to thinking that much of the educational system and many management techniques aim for: the search for a single right answer. Often there are several possible answers and before you decide on which one is right for your situation, you have to get as many of the possibilities out in the open as you can.

Sometimes brainstorming is thought to be just a group of people throwing ideas about, but when it is done in a disciplined way there are some rules to it.

Brainstorming rules

- Specify clearly a problem or a question and make sure it is understood in the same way by everyone. Then you need one person to stand at a flip-chart, or white board, and act as recorder and controller. Their primary job is to write down what everyone says, without changing it in any way; even if two people say almost the same thing, write them both down. Their other job is to enforce the rules that follow.

Phase 1 People call out their ideas, which can be as wacky as they like.

- Nobody is allowed to criticise or praise what someone else has said, it goes down exactly as called out without any evaluation of its suitability or feasibility. (This is an important rule for the recorder to enforce.)

- Whatever is called out gets written down, *verbatim*.

Phase 2 At the end of the first phase you have line after line of ideas on the board. The recorder leads the team in grouping together any ideas with a common thread; in the paper clip example which follows shortly, there would be all those that use the clip as a tool, for instance.

Phase 3 The team then goes through and agrees which ideas are completely unrealistic, and they get crossed off. The remaining ideas are then discussed and evaluated using whatever criteria the team sets for the task. You end up with a range of possible ideas that then can be refined down to one or two really workable options.

Any ideas produced in this way come from the team, are owned by the team and harness every scrap of creative thinking that exists.

Action point

Get the rules very clear in your mind, so tomorrow you can try it out with your team, using a common example which is, what uses are there for a paper clip?

The results can be quite astounding, as you'll see when you try it. The creativity triggered off by being encouraged to think outside the normal 'sensible' boundaries at work or by one person sparking off a related idea in someone else can be really useful in what it produces. However, more importantly, it puts the creative emphasis on the whole team and gets them involved right at the centre. The value of the session far exceeds its problem-solving dimension.

Another approach which helps people to share the information and knowledge they have – and sometimes don't even realise they have – is a technique we'll call 'collage' , because it builds up a picture from various scraps of material.

Collage

This is a procedure with two stages, individual and team. You can use just the second stage, but it really adds worthwhile thinking time if you build in stage 1 as well.

Collage rules

1   Put together 10 factual questions on a topic everybody knows something about, pop music in the '80s or Health and Safety rules, for instance.

2   Try and make a few of the questions multi-part, so the team members might get some parts right but not all.

3   Prepare a question sheet for each team member and an answer sheet, to use later.

4   Get individuals to tackle the questions alone, with no conferring at all, within a reasonable time limit.

5   Then, in a longer time limit (as discussion takes longer) get them to come up with answers the whole team accepts.

6 Finally, give them the answers so they can mark their individual answers and the team's answer. Be strict about marking, they must be right or score nothing.

Invariably, the team gets far more right than any individual, except in the unusual event of someone being an expert on the topic. If you ask the team what this shows they will say things like:

We get better answers when we pool our knowledge.

What so-and-so said was nearly right, and it triggered the right answer in my brain.

I don't mind sharing what I know with them, it works both ways.

Action point

Start working on some questions – and the answers – so you can use the technique tomorrow with the team.

Collage helps narrow down all the available information in people's heads and add it to what other people know. It can produce some remarkable results.

I never would have guessed...
A team of taxi drivers using this technique worked on questions from the Highway Code. In the team was the 17-year-old daughter of the firm's owner, who ran the radio.

The drivers clearly thought she wouldn't get many right and they looked a bit smug, even patronising. But when the questions were marked her individual score was the highest, and all the drivers admitted freely that she had played the major part in helping the team get a high score. They said it had been an eye-opener; never assume someone can't make a really valuable contribution just because of your own assumptions and stereotypes.

While the drivers had forgotten much of what they knew, the girl who ran the radio was about to take her test, so she had been swotting up on the information.

Facts and decisions are likely to be of a higher quality then when teams use collage because more people are making contributions and adding information from their own knowledge and experience. The discipline of the technique, paradoxically, enables the team to channel its resources in an effective way.

Sometimes, though, a right answer is obscured under a mass of irrelevant detail. A team technique for helping with this issue is one we can call 'information overload'.

Information overload

Using this technique provides the opportunity to look at issues like the communication trap.

You can draw up your own example, but to save you time, one has been put together for you to use, if you prefer. It is designed ideally for seven people, so they have three pieces of information each. (If you have eight or nine in your team you could give a few people two pieces of information or you could get a couple of the team members to act as observers and give feedback on how the process went, at the end.)

If you have fewer than seven, give out extra pieces of information to team members. They should all have roughly the same number of cards.

Because you know what is happening, you need to stay out of this activity. Don't be tempted to intervene or you will introduce an unfair advantage.

Information overload rules
Type out (or print) the following brief to give to everyone in the team.

At six o'clock on Tuesday, March 4, seventy people left their homes in the village of Ladchester to go to a leisure activity. How many went to see the hypnotist?

Now write the separate pieces of information shown opposite on separate cards.

To start the activity, mix up the cards so they are entirely random, and give them out to the team. Their task is to answer the question in the brief. You do nothing else.

The only leisure activities on Tuesdays are football, karate, and anything on at the Village Hall.	Tuesday evening is training night for the Ladchester Rovers Football Club First XI and their two reserves.
Jones is a builder, with a pick-up truck.	There is a talk at the Village Hall tonight.
The Horse & Hounds is five hundred yards from the Village Hall.	All events at the Village Hall start at 7.00 prompt.
The Rovers trainer lives in the village.	The football team faces relegation.
The Village Hall was built in 1923 from charitable donations.	The Karate Club is preparing for an international competition.
The three who went to the pub left together at 6.45.	The football trainer used to play for Arsenal, years ago.
The Village Hall speaker is a hypnotist.	The hypnotist has three grandchildren.
No hypnotists live in the village.	Hypnotism is an ancient art.
Smith and King never miss their Tuesday Karate Club, at 7.15.	Jones, King and Smith got to the Horse & Hounds at 6.15 and went in.
Jones has been looking forward to seeing the hypnotist for weeks.	The Horse & Hounds is in the Good Beer Guide.
Ladchester has 2,234 inhabitants.	

The answer is really quite simple. It is 54. Smith and King go to karate, the trainer, plus eleven players and two reserves go football training. However, in getting to the answer all sorts of things will happen in the team. They will possibly:

- Launch into action and start shouting out what they have on their cards, without planning how to handle the task, demonstrating the need for a conductor to make sure the aim is clear and procedures work
- Ignore the odd comment from someone about how to get the answer
- Demonstrate several examples of falling into the communication trap
- Start to make judgements about what they *assume* is irrelevant information, with no criteria to judge it by
- Agonise over what is *really* irrelevant information, in case they miss something

- Realise after a few minutes that they need a structure, at which point someone will take control and lead the procedures to their logical conclusion

If your team manages to avoid these pitfalls, congratulate them. Teams, once they have worked through it, tend to do much better the next time, and learn from their mistakes, as long as they have the chance to review what happened. In short, teams evolve and improve through practical endeavour and commitment.

Summary

The techniques we have looked at today will help establish some clear procedures for the team. Tomorrow, we will bring together all the issues we have looked at so far and use them to help the team review where it is and what it needs to do for its own development. If you are unclear about any of the issues or techniques covered earlier in the week, go back now and refresh your memory, so you are ready for tomorrow.

We can do better than this

Today we will bring together all the issues and points we have looked at over the week, and share them with the team. The first thing we're going to look at today is a sort of map, to take you through the initial process of identifying where you are now and where you want to be, clarifying what improvements can be made. Once you have a clear picture, you can take the rest of the team on the same journey, using the same map.

Later in the day you will see how important it is, once this initial teambuilding stage has been tackled, to keep an eye on how things are going, so you can make small adjustments that help the team develop further.

Aren't we good?

You may be very good, but this question implies complacency and satisfaction with things as they are. A better question is, 'how well do we match the quality standard we're aiming for?' The quality standard for teams is the ideal team, operating in the ideal way, and we have spent the last week exploring this.

Unless you believe your team is of perfect quality, there is always room for improvement. If you do believe it couldn't be improved you're either, **(a)** very lucky, **(b)** such an effective team leader you didn't need to open this book, or (most likely) **(c)** kidding yourself.

Any current management topic – from Total Quality Management to Customer Service to Just-in-Time – has a quality content and depends on teams. The need for an effective team always figures high on the list of essential characteristics. Another point that always appears is that quality is about continuous improvement, rather than a one-off quick fix; you can always do better!

In other words, there is a cycle of questions you need to have answered as you work to improve the quality of your team.

Where should we be?

You have started to answer this by the work you have done on:

- Leadership
- Aims
- Team roles
- Openness and honesty
- Procedures

Where should the team's results be?
This is fairly easy to assess, as long as you built in some objectives that provide a yardstick against which to measure the results. If an objective was

To produce the plan for the garden by the end of August

it's an open-and-shut case. You either did or you didn't. All objectives should have this measurability built in, as you know.

Because this is easier, and because the first task with a team is to focus on its development, while it is still young and impressionable, the emphasis during the rest of today is on the process, the how rather than the what.

What should the team's process be?
How the team works is hard to quantify, but the impression you now have of what makes a successful team is the best quality standard you can define. It isn't measurable in terms of numbers or product specifications, but it's like what someone once called 'the elephant test'.

It's almost impossible to describe an elephant, but you know what one looks like and you recognise it when you see it.

The elephant test is good enough. It provides you with a model in your head of what your team would look like if it were doing absolutely everything right every time. Trust your intuitive judgement on this – but don't be complacent.

Where are we now?

This is something you started to look at on Monday, when you completed that short check-list at the end, and set some initial priorities. What you did then was take an overall view of all the important characteristics, before you looked at each one in turn.

> **Action point**
>
> Explain to the team about the overview you looked at on Monday, and give them a copy of the check-list to complete. Live with the fact that, at this stage, they might not be as clued up as you are about the details of each characteristic. Just get the broad feel for where everybody thinks the team is now.

What are the gaps?

Depending on what sort of scores everybody comes up with, you can assess together where the priorities lie, and these are the biggest gaps.

Naturally, there will be different perceptions around the team, so an open discussion is likely to be needed. It is quite likely that one reason for very different scores is individuals' unique interpretations of what the words mean, and getting into the detail of each characteristic may be the only way of sorting out any such confusion. So, if there are still very different views, ask people to hold on to them. Explain that they will get the chance to look at the check-list again later, after they have explored what each of the characteristics means.

How do we close the gaps?

The first step is to check back and make sure that any item
on the check-list that looks as if it isn't in need of attention
really is OK. Remember, at this stage the team members
haven't looked at the openness and honesty issues and so,
for instance, they may say you're a brilliant leader because
they think that's what they ought to say. You might feel just
like one of the team, but if you're the senior person there,
the others will always have in the back of their minds that
you're the boss.

So ask some probing questions before you decide to accept
any issue as being healthy enough to leave for now. You
may need to be self-critical about this, too. Then, once you
have identified the most important priority, you as the team
leader can relay to the rest of the team what lies behind the
issue, using the work you did through the week.

If you look back, you'll see that on each day you have been asked to do something that you can now ask them to do. The aim has always been to provide you with a chance to build in some resources you can use to cascade your knowledge and understanding to the rest of the team.

In addition to using the materials you have worked through, there are several other options. They include:

- Asking the team to come up with solutions and ways forward for themselves
- Getting in a consultant to help you focus on team development
- Buying one of the many sets of teambuilding exercises that are on the market

A starter for 10

It doesn't really matter where you start. So, if you have several priorities you could decide to have a look at team roles first, because that is a topic that automatically gets everyone involved and starts them talking. Or you may prefer to start with procedures, simply because you have a set of ready-made activities from yesterday that you can see.

On the other hand, if you start with openness and honesty, you could sort out the ground rules before doing anything else. What matters is starting somewhere – anywhere – rather than getting caught in analysis paralysis and looking for the one right answer that doesn't exist. Go for it!

Back to the beginning

Once you have looked at all the important issues, go back to the original checklist and either get everyone to do it again, or let them see whether they want to reconsider their initial thoughts. This will either confirm or change the top priorities, and ensure that you're devoting your energies to the appropriate areas. It may mean going back and filling in any previously hidden gaps, but better to do it now than leave something undone.

Keeping an eye on things

So, you have taken the first step and worked with the team to look at where it is now and where it wants to be. You have identified the gaps and planned some action to get you across them.

However, this is only the beginning. Like a child growing up, the team is starting to develop and mature, but it has a long way to go. It still needs attention to detail, so it can keep on developing, rather than staying an adolescent.

Dangerous results

The team starts working and it begins to focus on achieving its aims and objectives. At this point there is a danger, which is that the 'what', the results, takes over all the attention from the 'how', the process.

Another cycle can help here, because it gives you three simple questions to ask, whenever there is the chance to spend a few minutes reviewing progress.

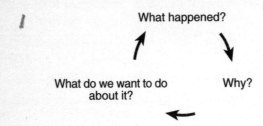

Asking these simple questions is a process you have seen several times during the week, especially when the notion of someone observing the team and giving feedback appeared. This time, though, the team members themselves ask and answer the questions.

There is a variation you might like to use, by breaking down the 'what happened' question into:

- What went well?
- What went badly?

An example of the answers might look like this. First, something that went badly.

Team review
What went well?
We got the decision sorted out and everybody agrees, even though a couple of us were not originally keen.

Why?
Because we accepted we're in this together and it has to be the best possible compromise. We overcame some fairly major differences that would have stopped us in the past.

What do we want to do about it?
Celebrate this success, and do it again next time.

There are a couple of important points here:

> - Success is worth celebrating because it:
> - confirms things are going well and the team has done the right things
> - gives people a good feeling
> - breeds further success.
> - It is worth reviewing what went well because it clarifies it is something to do again.

Team review
What went badly?
Derek opted out of the discussion on the timetable.

Why?
Claire and David both snapped at him and wouldn't listen to his point of view. It was getting late by then and we were all a bit tired.

What do we want to do about it?
Alison, as the conductor, needs to jump on situations like that more quickly. Claire and David need to remember the ground rules, so does Derek, who should have been more assertive. Also, we should take a few short breaks so we don't all get so stressed.

Using a simple and short review technique like this will help ensure that all the work you have done is not eroded by time.

And now, the review process when things go well.

Building and maintaining a team is not easy and it doesn't happen on its own, but if you get everyone involved in working out where they want to improve, and how, you will inevitably find you and the other members are part of a successful team, and a very satisfying experience.

Summary

Today, we have brought together all the issues and points that we have looked at through the week. Now, the real work begins when you start putting all this into practice. Don't expect to find the 'answers' in this guide – teamwork is an activity that happens in the real world! Remember your priorities and don't get distracted.

NOTES

NOTES

Further *Successful Business in a Week* **titles from Hodder & Stoughton and the Institute of Management all at £6.99**

All Hodder & Stoughton books are available from your local bookshop or can be ordered direct from the publisher. Just tick the titles you want and fill in the form below. Prices and availability subject to change without notice.

To: Hodder & Stoughton Ltd, Cash Sales Department, Bookpoint, 39 Milton Park, Abingdon, Oxon, OX14 4TD. If you have a credit card you may order by telephone – 01235 400414.

E-mail address: orders@bookpoint.co.uk

Please enclose a cheque or postal order made payable to Bookpoint Ltd to the value of the cover price and allow the following for postage and packaging:

UK & BFPO: £4.30 for one book; £6.30 for two books; £8.30 for three books.

OVERSEAS & EIRE: £4.80 for one book; £7.10 for 2 or 3 books (surface mail).

Name: ....

Address: ....

....

If you would prefer to pay by credit card, please complete:

Please debit my Visa/Mastercard/Diner's Card/American Express (delete as appropriate) card no:

☐☐☐☐☐☐☐☐☐☐☐☐☐☐☐☐☐☐

Signature .... Expiry Date ....